RECONSTRUCTING AMERICA 1865-1890

STUDENT STUDY GUIDE

OXFORD

UNIVERSITY PRESS

OXFORD
UNIVERSITY PRESS

Oxford University Press, Inc., publishes works that
further Oxford University's objective of excellence
in research, scholarship, and education.

Oxford   New York
Auckland   Cape Town   Dar es Salaam   Hong Kong   Karachi
Kuala Lumpur   Madrid   Melbourne   Mexico City   Nairobi
New Delhi   Shanghai   Taipei   Toronto

With offices in
Argentina   Austria   Brazil   Chile   Czech Republic   France   Greece
Guatemala   Hungary   Italy   Japan   Poland   Portugal   Singapore
South Korea   Switzerland   Thailand   Turkey   Ukraine   Vietnam

Published by Oxford University Press, Inc.
198 Madison Avenue, New York, NY 10016
www.oup.com

Oxford is a registered trademark of Oxford University Press

ISBN-13: 978-0-19-522322-4 (California edition)   ISBN-13: 978-0-19-518886-8
ISBN-10: 0-19-522322-5 (California edition)   ISBN-10: 0-19-518886-1

Writer: Scott Ingram
Project Manager: Matt Fisher
Project Director: Jacqueline A. Ball
Education Consultant: Diane L. Brooks, Ed.D.
Design: designlabnyc

Casper Grathwohl, Publisher

Printed in the United States of America
on acid-free paper

Dear Parents, Guardians, and Students:

This study guide has been created to increase student enjoyment and understanding of *A History of US*.

The study guide offers a wide variety of interactive exercises to support every chapter. At the back of the guide are maps to help tie the study of history to the study of geography. (Corresponding activities appear in the teaching guide for this book.) Also at the back of the guide are several copies of a library/media center research log students can use to organize research projects and assignments. Parents or other family members can participate in activities marked "With a Parent or Partner." Adults can help in other ways, too. One important way is to encourage students to create and use a history journal as they work through the exercises in the guide. The journal can simply be an off-the-shelf notebook or three-ring binder used only for this purpose. Some students might like to customize their journals with markers, colored paper, drawings, or computer graphics. No matter what it looks like, a journal is a student's very own place to organize thoughts, practice writing, and make notes on important information. It will serve as a personal report of ongoing progress that your child's teacher can evaluate regularly. When completed, it will be a source of satisfaction and accomplishment for your child.

Sincerely,

Casper Grathwohl
Publisher

This book belongs to:

_____

CONTENTS

Bosses such as William Marcy Tweed built political machines that lay outside the system of checks and balances set up by the Constitution. Nonetheless, they found themselves checked by another nongovernmental power—the scathing pen of political cartoonist Thomas Nast.

HOW TO USE THE
STUDENT STUDY GUIDES TO
A HISTORY OF US

One word describes A History of US: stories. Every book in this series is packed with stories about people who built a brand new country like none before. You will meet presidents and politicians, artists and inventors, ordinary people who did amazing things and had wonderful adventures. The best part is that all the stories are true. All the people are real.

As you read this book, you can enjoy the stories while you build valuable thinking and writing skills. The book will help you pass important tests. The sample pages below show special features in all the History of US books. Take a look!

Before you read

- Have a notebook or extra paper and a pen handy to make a history journal. A dictionary and thesaurus will help you too.

- Read the chapter title and predict what you will learn from the chapter. Note that often the author often adds humor to her titles with plays on words or **puns**, as in this title.

- Study all maps, photos, and their captions closely. The captions often contain important information you won't find in the text.

A HISTORY OF US

27 *Howe Billy Wished France Wouldn't Join In*

A **hoop-stay** was part of the stiffening in a skirt; a **japon** was part of a corset. **Matrons** are married women. The **misses** are single girls; **swains** and **beaux** are young men or boyfriends. **Making love** meant flirting. **British Grenadiers** are part of the royal household's infantry.

General Howe had already served in America. In 1759 he led Wolfe's troops to seize Quebec.

Sir William Howe (who was sometimes called Billy Howe) was in charge of all the British forces in America. It was Howe who drove the American army from Long Island to Manhattan. Then he chased it across another river to New Jersey. And, after that, he forced George Washington to flee on—to Pennsylvania. It looked as if it was all over for the rebels. In New Jersey, some 3,000 Americans took an oath of allegiance to the king. But Washington got lucky again. The Europeans didn't like to fight in cold weather.

Sir William settled in New York City for the winter season. Howe thought Washington and his army were done for and could be

Swarming with Beaux

Rebecca Franks was the daughter of a wealthy Philadelphia merchant. Her father was the king's agent in Pennsylvania, and the family were Loyalists. Rebecca visited New York when it was occupied by the British. Her main interest in the war was that it meant New York was full of handsome officers:

My Dear Abby, By the by, few New York ladies know how to entertain company in their own houses unless they introduce the card tables....I don't know a woman or girl that can chat above half an hour, and that on the form of a cap, the colour of a ribbon or the set of a hoop-stay or jupon....Here, you enter a room with a formal set curtsey and after the how do's, 'tis a fine, or a bad day, and those trifling nothings are finish'd, all's a dead calm till the cards are introduced, when you see pleasure dancing in the eyes of all the matrons....The misses, if they have a favorite swain, frequently decline playing for the pleasure of making love....Yesterday the Grenadiers had a race at the Flatlands, and in the afternoon this house swarm'd with beaux and some very smart ones. How the girls wou'd have envy'd me cou'd they have peep'd and seen how I was surrounded.

126

As you read

- Keep a list of questions.

- Note the bold-faced definitions in the margins. They tell you the meanings of important words and terms – ones you may not know.

- Look up other unfamiliar words in a dictionary.

- Note other sidebars or special features. They contain additional information for your enjoyment and to build your understanding. Often sidebars and features contain quotations from primary source documents such as a diary or letter, like this one. Sometimes the primary source item is a cartoon or picture.

After you read

- Compare what you have learned with what you thought you would learn before you began the chapter.

The next two pages have models of graphic organizers. You will need these to do the activities for each chapter on the pages after that. Go back to the book as often as you need to.

finished off in springtime. Besides, Billy Howe loved partying. And some people say he liked the Americans and didn't approve of George III's politics. For reasons that no one is quite sure of, General Howe just took it easy.

But George Washington was no quitter. On Christmas Eve of 1776, in bitter cold, Washington got the Massachusetts fishermen to ferry his men across the Delaware River from Pennsylvania back to New Jersey. The river was clogged with huge chunks of ice. You had to be crazy, or coolly courageous, to go out into that dangerous water. The Hessians, on the other side—at Trenton, New Jersey—were so sure Washington wouldn't cross in such bad weather that they didn't patrol the river. Washington took them by complete surprise.

A week later, Washington left a few men to tend his campfires and fool the enemy. He quietly marched his army to Prince-ton, New Jersey, where he surprised and beat a British force. People in New Jersey forgot the oaths they had sworn to the king. They were Patriots again.

Those weren't big victories that Washington had won, but they certainly helped American morale. And American morale needed help. It still didn't seem as if the colonies had a chance. After all, Great Britain had the most feared army in the world. It was amazing that a group of small colonies would even attempt to fight the powerful British empire. When a large English army (9,500 men and 138 cannons) headed south from Canada in June 1777, many observers thought the rebellion would soon be over.

The army was led by one of Britain's

General Burgoyne's redcoats carried far too much equipment. Each man's boots alone weighed 12 pounds. They took two months to cover 40 miles from Fort Ticonderoga to Saratoga, and lost hundreds of men to American snipers.

127

7

GRAPHIC ORGANIZERS

As you read and study history, geography, and the social sciences, you'll start to collect a lot of information. Using a graphic organizer is one way to make information clearer and easier to understand. You can choose from different types of organizers, depending on the information.

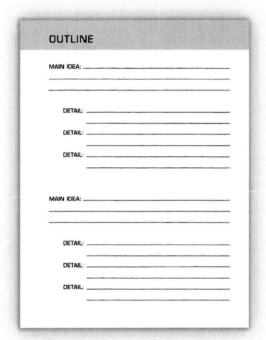

Outline

To build an outline, first identify your main idea. Write this at the top. Then, in the lines below, list the details that support the main idea. Keep adding main ideas and details as you need to.

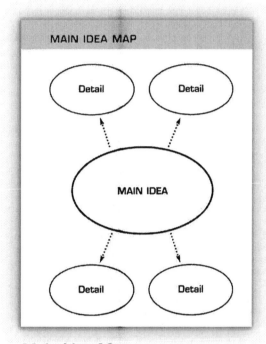

Main Idea Map

Write down your main idea in the central circle. Write details in the connecting circles.

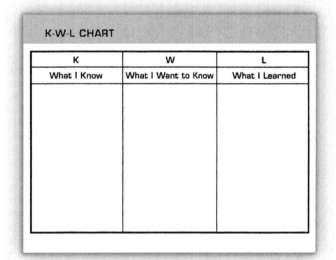

K-W-L Chart

Before you read a chapter, write down what you already know about a subject in the left column. Then write what you want to know in the center column. Then write what you learned in the last column. You can make a two-column version of this. Write what you know in the left and what you learned after reading the chapter.

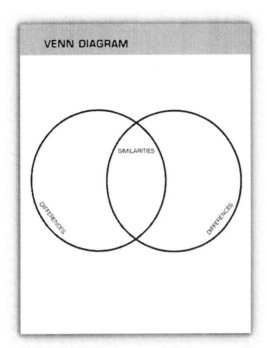

Venn Diagram

These overlapping circles show differences and similarities among topics. Each topic is shown as a circle. Any details the topics have in common go in the areas where those circles overlap. List the differences where the circles do not overlap.

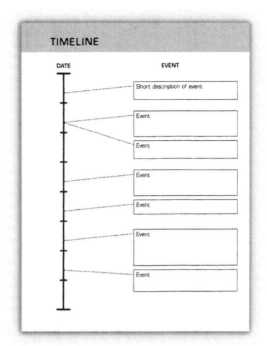

Timeline

A timeline divides a time period into equal chunks of time. Then it shows when events happened during that time. Decide how to divide up the timeline. Then write events in the boxes to the right when they happened. Connect them to the date line.

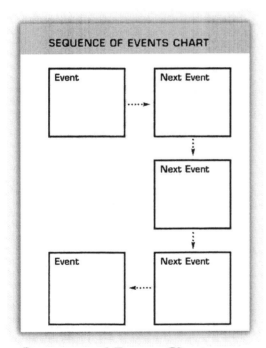

Sequence of Events Chart

Historical events bring about changes. These result in other events and changes. A sequence of events chart uses linked boxes to show how one event leads to another, and then another.

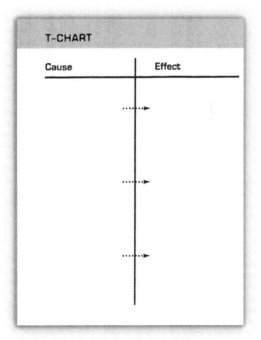

T-Chart

Use this chart to separate information into two columns. To separate causes and effects, list events, or causes, in one column. In the other column, list the change, or effect, each event brought about.

REPORTS AND SPECIAL PROJECTS

Aside from the activities in this Study Guide, your teacher may ask you to do some extra research or reading about American history on your own. Or, you might become interested in a particular story you read in *A History of US* and want to find out more. Do you know where to start?

GETTING STARTED

The back of every History of US book has a section called "More Books to Read." Some of these books are fiction and some are nonfiction. This list is different for each book in the series. When you want to find out more about a particular topic from the reading, these books are a great place to start—and you should be able to find all of them in your school library.

Also, if you're specifically looking for *primary sources*, you can start with the *History of US Sourcebook and Index*. This book is full of *primary sources*, words and evidence about history directly from the people who were involved. This is an excellent place to find the exact words from important speeches and documents.

DOING RESEARCH

For some of the group projects and assignments in this course, you will need to conduct research either in a library or online. When your teacher asks you to research a topic, remember the following tips:

TO FIND GOOD EVIDENCE, START WITH GOOD SOURCES

Usually, your teacher will expect you to support your research with *primary sources*. Remember that a primary source for an event comes from someone who was there when the even took place. The best evidence for projects and writing assignments always comes from *primary sources*, so if you can't seem to find any right away, keep looking.

ASK THE LIBRARIAN

Librarians are amazing people who can help you find just about anything in the library. If you can't seem to find what you're looking for, remember to ask a librarian for help.

WHEN RESEARCHING ONLINE, STICK TO CREDIBLE WEBSITES

It can be difficult to decide which websites are credible and which are not. To be safe, stick with websites that both you and your teacher trust. There are plenty of online sources that have information you can trust to be correct, and usually they're names you already know. For example, you can trust the facts you get from places like pbs.org, census.gov, historychannel.com, and historyofus.com. In addition to free websites like these, check with your librarian to see which *databases and subscription-based websites* your school can access.

USE THE LIBRARY/MEDIA CENTER RESEARCH LOG

At the back of this study guide, you'll find several copies of a Library/Media Center Research Log. Take one with you to the library or media center, and keep track of your sources. Also, take time to decide how helpful and relevant those sources are.

OTHER RESOURCES

Your school and public library have lots of additional resources to help you with your research. These include videos, DVDs, software, and CDs.

RECONSTRUCTING MEANS REBUILDING

SUMMARY *The Civil War destroyed a way of life in the South. President Lincoln had hoped to reconstruct the region with a gentle hand. But his assassination deprived the nation of the patience and wisdom needed to heal its deep spiritual wounds.*

ACCESS

To help understand the conditions in the South after the Civil War, make a K-W-L graphic organizer in your history journal like the one on page 9. In the "What I *Know*" column write what you know about what the South was like after the Civil War ended. In the "What I *Want* to Know" column, write five questions you have about the war's aftermath. After you read the chapter, fill out the "What I *Learned*" column with answers to your questions and other information.

WORD BANK   polyglot   Reconstruction   artificial

Complete the sentences below with words from the word bank. One word is not used.

1. _Reconstruction_ was a time of great uncertainty in the South about the direction of their society.
2. A _polyglot_ city is one in which many languages are spoken.

CRITICAL THINKING MAKING INFERENCES

Put S in the blank if the statement below reflects the point of view of a Southerner. Put N if the statement reflects the point of view of a Northerner. Put E if the statement reflects a point of view of either a Southerner or a Northerner.

_E_ 1. The Civil War was over, and all across the land mothers and fathers buried their sons.

_N_ 2. After all, it was the South that had started the war.

_N_ 3. Some thought the Rebel leaders should be hanged.

_S_ 4. Their lovely, elegant, aristocratic society was in ruins.

_S_ 5. Everything they had fought for seemed gone.

_E_ 6. Guerrilla bands looted at will.

_S_ 7. As for the Civil War itself, all they had tried to do, they said, was form their own nation.

_E_ 8. Someone needed to do some organizing.

WORKING WITH PRIMARY SOURCES

Read the words of Mark Twain below. In your history journal, write complete sentences to answer the questions.

> The war is the great chief topic of conversation. The interest in it is vivid and constant; the interest in other topics is fleeting . . . In the South, the war is what A.D. is elsewhere: they date from it.

1. What does the word *vivid* mean in the statement above?
2. From reading the words above, why do you think interest in other topics was "fleeting"?
3. What do the letters A.D. mean in the statement above?
4. What does "they date from it" mean in the statement above?

WRITING

Imagine you are a Rebel soldier returning home to a city that resembles the photograph on page 13. You have been away for several years. Write a diary entry in your history journal about the experience.

WHO WAS ANDREW JOHNSON?
PRESIDENTIAL RECONSTRUCTION

SUMMARY *Andrew Johnson had shown courage when he turned his back on sectionalism and chose loyalty to the Union instead. But his stubborn, uncompromising nature proved his undoing as President. The Freedmen's Bureau attempted to help African Americans adjust to their new lives. But in some people's eyes, President Johnson was not doing enough to protect freed people.*

ACCESS

Copy the main idea map on page 8 into your history journal. In the largest circle, write the word *Reconstruction*. Use each of the smaller circles to write facts about that period, including a circle about Andrew Johnson.

WORD BANK   Seward's Folly   compromise   traitor   martial law   black codes   freedmen

Complete the sentences below with words from the word bank. One word is not used.

1. Some Americans described the purchase of Alaska as _Seward's Folly_.
2. Many Northerners felt that Alexander Stephens, the vice president of the Confederacy, was a _traitor_.
3. Southerners passed laws called the _black codes_ to take rights away from African Americans.
4. Few people in the North or South wanted to _compromise_, or cooperate with one another.
5. Much of the South was under _martial law_, with soldiers in control of the region.

CRITICAL THINKING   FACT OR OPINION

A fact is a statement that can be proven. An opinion judges things or people but cannot be proved or disproved. Put F or O in front of the sentences below from the chapter.

___O___ 1. People didn't know quite what to expect of President Andrew Johnson.

___F___ 2. He was in the Senate when the Southern states, including Tennessee, seceded.

___O___ 3. Andrew Johnson was uncompromising.

___F___ 4. Congress had created a Freedmen's Bureau even before the war had ended.

___F___ 5. Thousands of Southerners left the country for Mexico and South America.

___F___ 6. And, once again, they turned to short-sighted leaders.

WORKING WITH PRIMARY SOURCES

Read the words of Charlotte Forten below. In your history journal, answer the questions that follow with complete sentences.

> I have not had half as many scholars as usual. It was too cold for my 'babies' to venture out. But . . . [t]hey were unusually bright today, and sang with the greatest spirit.

1. What does the word *scholars* mean in the statement above?
2. Why does Forten call the children "babies"?
3. What does the word *bright* mean in the sentence?
4. Do you think Forten enjoyed teaching? Why or why not?

WRITING

Look at the political cartoons in the chapter. In your history journal, answer the following.

1. What would people say today if a president was drawn as a parrot or as a Roman emperor?
2. Why was Andrew Johnson shown as a tailor?
3. How do you think people in the South would feel being pictured as naughty children?

SLAVERY AND STATE'S RIGHTS

SUMMARY *Two amendments to the Constitution addressed the issues over which the Civil War was fought. The 13th Amendment abolished slavery, and the 14th Amendment limited states' rights and made the federal government the guardian of individual liberties.*

ACCESS

This chapter discusses the aftermath of the Civil War and the challenges that faced African Americans. In your history journal, make a cause and effect chart like the one on page 9. For the first cause, write "The 13th Amendment was ratified in 1865." List the effect. What was the cause that resulted from the first effect? Fill in at least five cause-and-effect relationships with information from the chapter.

WORD BANK   nullify   unalienable (inalienable)   states' rights   civil rights   veto

Complete the sentences below with words from the word bank. One word is not used.

1. The term _unalienable_, not pronounced _inalienable_, was used by Thomas Jefferson to describe a kind of right in the Declaration of Independence.

2. Many Southern supported the idea of _states' rights_, which allowed states to _veto_ laws that they felt went against the interests of their state.

3. African Americans and Radical Republicans felt that the Constitution should be amended to guarantee the _civil rights_ of all citizens against state laws.

CRITICAL THINKING SEQUENCE OF EVENTS

The sentences below describe the events in the battle for equal treatment. Put 1, 2, 3, and so on in front of the sentences that describe what happened.

___6___ Radical Republicans in Congress pass the Civil Rights Act to prohibit the Black Codes.

___5___ The 13th Amendment abolishing slavery is ratified. *1865*

___7___ President Johnson vetoes the Civil Rights Act.

___1___ Thomas Jefferson writes the Declaration of Independence

___4___ Southern states pass the black codes.   *but a*

___3___ The Civil War is fought to end slavery.

___2___ The Constitution and the Bill of Rights are ratified.

___8___ The 14th Amendment is ratified. *1868*

WORKING WITH PRIMARY SOURCES

Read the words of the 14th Amendment below. In your history journal, answer the questions that follow.

> No State shall deprive any person of life, liberty, or property, without due process of law; nor deny to any person within its jurisdiction the equal protection of the laws.

1. What does the word *deprive* mean in the statement above?

2. What is the "due process of law"?

3. What does the word *jurisdiction* mean?

4. What is another way to say "equal protection of the laws"?

5. Brainstorm a few ways to say life, liberty, or property" in your own words.

6. Rewrite the passage above in your own words, using your answers from questions 1-5.

CHAPTER 5

CONGRESSIONAL RECONSTRUCTION

SUMMARY *In 1867, Radical Republicans in Congress took control of Reconstruction. Federal troops marched South and opened the doors of government to newly enfranchised blacks.*

ACCESS

Make a K-W-L graphic organizer in your history journal like the one on page 9. In the "What I *Know*" column, write what you have learned so far about Reconstruction. Skim the chapter, looking at pictures, captions, and key words. In the "What I *Want* to Know" column, write five questions you have about Reconstruction. After you read the chapter, fill out the "What I *Learned*" column.

WORD BANK   interests   illiterate   integrity

Complete the sentences below with words from the word bank. One word is not used.

1. A person who is true to his or her beliefs has _integrity_.
2. A person who is unable to read and write is _illiterate_.

CRITICAL THINKING DRAWING CONCLUSIONS

Each of the sentences in *italics* below is taken from the chapter. Put a check mark in front of all of the conclusions that can be drawn from reading the lines.

1. *Congress decided to send soldiers south to guarantee freedom to the former slaves.*

_____ (a) Congress sent only black soldiers.

__✓__ (b) Former slaves had difficulty gaining their freedom from their owners.

__✓__ (c) Bitterness between Southern whites and blacks remained after the war.

2. *Some observers burst into cheers to see a black as a senator.*

__✓__ (a) Black men were not elected to Congress before the Civil War.

_____ (b) Southerners were the people who burst into cheers.

__✓__ (c) Not everyone cheered during the event.

3. *And no women were elected at all—north or south—because women still couldn't vote.*

__✓__ (a) African American men were able to vote before women.

_____ (b) Women at the time did not want to vote.

__✓__ (c) Most men in both the North and South agreed that women should not vote.

MAP

Study the map on page 26. In your history journal, answer the questions that follow.

1. Was West Virginia readmitted to the Union? Why or why not?

2. Which Confederate state was the first to be readmitted to the Union?

3. In which year were the most states readmitted to the Union?

4. Which states were the last to be readmitted to the Union?

WORKING WITH PRIMARY SOURCES

Study the cartoon of the "three pillars of the Democratic Party" on page 25. Decide which of the three figures is the immigrant.

1. Which is the "Rebel?"

2. Which is the Wall Street financier?

3. What is the opinion of the cartoonist about the Democratic Party?

Write some notes in your history journal.

THADDEUS STEVENS: RADICAL

SUMMARY *Thaddeus Stevens's unrelenting and uncompromising resolve to win justice for African Americans led to the impeachment of President Andrew Johnson—one of the great trials in U.S. history.*

IMPEACHING A PRESIDENT

SUMMARY *The fate of President Johnson rested upon a single vote. In an act of courage, Senator Edmund Ross of Kansas voted against impeachment and in favor of preserving the balance between Congress and the presidency.*

ACCESS

This chapter discusses two bitter enemies, Thaddeus Stevens and Andrew Johnson. To organize the information as you read, make a Venn diagram graphic organizer in your history journal like the one on page 9. In one circle, list the facts that you learn about Thaddeus Stevens from the chapter. In the other circle, list things that you learn about Andrew Johnson. In the area where the two circles intersect, list the qualities that the men had in common.

WORD BANK   impeach   high crimes   misdemeanors   moderate   conviction   bigotry   balance of power

Complete the sentences below with words from the word bank. One word is not used.

1. Representatives who vote to ___*impeach*___ a president are voting to charge him with misconduct.
2. ___*high crimes*___ are illegal acts that endanger the security of the country.
3. ___*misdemeanors*___ are illegal acts that bring dishonor to the offices of the presidency.
4. The responsibilities shared by the three branches of the government mean that our nation is governed with a ___*balance of power*___
5. People who discriminate against others because of their race are guilty of ___*bigotry*___.
6. Ross, who voted based on the evidence, was a person of strong ___*conviction*___.

CRITICAL THINKING MAKING INFERENCES

Put S if the sentence below refers to Thaddeus Stevens. Put J if the sentence refers to Andrew Johnson. Put B if it refers to both men.

___B___ 1. He thought strong laws were needed to make people behave properly.

___S___ 2. People called him an abolitionist—a name that was no help to a politician in that antebellum time.

___J___ 3. He seemed to stand against most Northerners, all blacks, and the moderate Southern Unionists.

___S___ 4. He was the chief author of the 14th Amendment.

___J___ 5. He was convinced that it was not the responsibility of the nation to help the newly freed men and women get equal treatment before the law.

WORKING WITH PRIMARY SOURCES

Read the words from the Constitution below. In your history journal, answer the questions that follow.

> The Senate shall have the sole Power to try all impeachments. . . . the Chief Justice shall preside and no Person shall be convicted without the Concurrence of two thirds of the members present.

1. If the Senate has the "Power" to "try all impeachments," what power does the House of Representatives have?

2. Who is the person referred to as the "Chief Justice"?

3. What is another word for "preside" in the statement?

4. What does the word "Concurrence" mean?

5. Today there are 100 Senators. How many votes would it take to vote a president out of office?

WELCOME TO MEETING STREET

SUMMARY *Reconstruction legislatures prompted some people to talk of "America's Second Revolution." Slowly but surely, former Confederate officers and officials organized "Redeemer" governments that pushed blacks out of politics.*

ACCESS

Make an outline in your history journal like the one on page 8. For the title, write *Reconstruction Legislature*. For main ideas, write *Government, Blacks, Whites,* and *Laws*. Include at least two details under each main idea.

WORD BANK   ubiquitous   redeemer   governments

Answer the questions below in complete sentences

1. Read the sidebar on page 36. Why do you think the author says that corruption was *ubiquitous* in American history?

Ubiquitous means everywhere — the America history is full of corruption from slavery

2. What sentence on page 39 explains the meaning of "redeemer governments"?

line 23 - call controlled by former Confederates.

3. Write a sentence that uses the word "ubiquitous."

Music is ubiquitous.

CRITICAL THINKING   MAIN IDEA AND SUPPORTING DETAILS

Each sentences in *italics* below states a main idea from the chapter. Put a check mark in the blank in front of the ONE sentence that DOES NOT support or tell more about the main idea.

1. *In their handsome, shuttered homes overlooking Charleston harbor, the city's white aristocrats wait and worry.*

_____ (a) Some of the old plantation families are worried.

___✓__ (b) Robert Brown Elliot is as well educated as anyone here.

_____ (c) Will the assembly demand revenge for the years of slavery?

2. *Some say this session is the beginning of "America's Second Revolution."*

___✓__ (a) It is an attempt at a genuine interracial society.

___✓__ (b) All across the South, Reconstruction legislatures are at work.

_____ (c) No question about it—this is government by the people.

3. *Most Southerners are small farmers. This is a terrible time for them.*

___✓__ (a) Six men in the Florida legislature cannot read or write.

_____ (b) Cotton prices have fallen to low levels.

_____ (c) As if that is not bad enough, the weather is poor and so are the harvests.

WRITING

What does the word *equal* mean to you? In your history journal, write down five thoughts that come to mind when you think of that word.

A SOUTHERN GIRL'S DIARY

SUMMARY *African Americans who had been enslaved, such as the Montgomery family, briefly tasted the joy of land ownership and free enterprise. Their success made the reconfiscation of lands by former Confederates even more bitter—and more unjust.*

ACCESS

Make a cause and effect chart in your history journal like the one on page 9. For the first cause, write "Joseph Davis sells property to Benjamin Montgomery." For the first effect write "Montgomery founds Davis Bend." What was the cause that resulted from the first effect? Fill in at least five cause-and-effect relationships.

WORD BANK   patent   subverted   model

Complete the sentences below with words from the word bank. One word is not used.

1. The Ku Klux Klan weakened, or ___subverted___, the rights of African Americans in Kentucky and other states.

2. A ___patent___ gives an inventor protection against others copying his invention without payment.

CRITICAL THINKING SEQUENCE OF EVENTS

The sentences from the chapter below describe the events in the chapter. Put 1, 2, 3, and so on in front of the sentences to put them in chronological order.

__4__ A year after the war's end, Joseph Davis sold two of his plantations to Mary Virginia's father, Benjamin Montgomery.

__1__ When the war was over, in 1865, Jefferson Davis was a hated man.

__3__ So when the Union army came into Mississippi and Joseph Davis fled, his slaves didn't go with him.

__8__ Mary Virginia had to move.

__6__ In 1870, Montgomery cotton won a prize as the best at the St. Louis Fair.

__7__ Now, seven years after the end of the war, he was in Mississippi, visiting his old plantation.

__5__ Freedmen and freedwomen flocked to Davis Bend.

__2__ Before the war he had ruled what he believed was an ideal plantation.

WORKING WITH PRIMARY SOURCES

Read the excerpt of the 1871 petition to Congress below. In your history journal, answer the questions that follow.

> We the colored citizens of Frankfort . . . state that life, liberty, and property are unprotected among the colored race of this state. Organized bands of desperate and lawless men, mainly composed of soldiers of the late Rebel armies, armed, disciplined, and disguised, and bound by oath and secret obligations, have by force, terror, and violence subverted all civil society . . .

1. What does the petition mean by "property"?

2. What does the petition mean by "subverted all civil society"?

3. What are the "Rebel armies" and why are they called "late"?

10

A FAILED REVOLUTION

SUMMARY *In 1877, a political deal led President Rutherford Hayes to call an end to Reconstruction. By the end of the decade, black Southerners found themselves under the lash of a new master—a fool named Jim Crow.*

ACCESS

This chapter discusses the series of events that led to the end of Reconstruction. In your history journal, make a cause and effect chart like the one on page 9. For the first cause write *Grant allows corrupt men to influence his government.* For the first effect write *Corruption made Americans forget about civil rights.* What was the cause that resulted from the first effect? Fill in at least five cause-and-effect relationships.

WORD BANK   sharecropping   poll tax   lynching   segregation   Jim Crow   harmony

Complete the sentences below with words from the word bank. One word is not used.

1. Carpetbaggers and blacks were threatened with ___lynching___ by Southern racists.
2. A ___segregation___ society is one in which the races are kept apart. In the South the laws that made this possible were name after a foolish character, ___Jim Crow___.
3. The ___poll tax___ was a way to making poor black pay to vote.
4. ___sharecropping___ allowed rich landowners to take the crops of poor farmers who "rented" land for planting.

CRITICAL THINKING DRAWING CONCLUSIONS

Each of the sentences in *italics* below is taken from the chapter. Put a check mark in front of all of the conclusions that can be drawn from reading the lines.

1. *During the Reconstruction period black lawmakers voted for schools, roads, and railroads.*

_____ (a) White lawmakers also voted for schools, roads, and railroads.

___✓___ (b) Blacks were able to vote during Reconstruction.

_____ (c) White people did not need schools, roads, and railroads.

2. *The United States was going from agrarian nation to industrial giant.*

___✓___ (a) Factories were replacing farms as workplaces.

_____ (b) Americans did not want to go from agriculture to industry.

___✓___ (c) The change in workplaces brought changes to society.

3. *When President Rutherford B. Hayes did what he had promised—he pulled the soldiers out of the South—congressional Reconstruction was just about finished.*

___✓___ (a) The President commanded the army.

___✓___ (b) Soldiers had been in the South to help Reconstruction take place.

_____ (c) Reconstruction was successful, so soldiers were no longer needed.

WORKING WITH PRIMARY SOURCES

Read the words of historian Eric Foner below. In your history journal, answer the questions that follow.

> 1877 marked a decisive retreat from the idea, born during the Civil War, of a powerful nation state protecting the fundamental rights of American citizens.

1. From reading the chapter, what "retreat" took place in 1877?
2. What does Foner mean by a "powerful nation state"?
3. What are "fundamental rights"?
4. Who are the "American citizens" about whom Foner is writing?

MEANWHILE, OUT WEST

SUMMARY *No sooner had the Civil War ended than settlers spilled onto the Great Plains. Here settlers battled Native Americans and the environment to turn the prairies into the nation's "breadbasket."*

RIDING THE TRAIL

SUMMARY *For a brief period, much of the Great Plains belonged to the Texas longhorns and cattle herders who rode the open range. The meeting of cattle trails and railroad lines created "cow towns' still famous in western lore—Abilene, Dodge City, Wichita, and others.*

ACCESS

These chapters describe events west of the Mississippi after the Civil War. To help understand the importance of farming, cattle, and settlers, make a K-W-L graphic organizer in your history journal like the one on page 9. In the "What I *Know*" column write what you know about the settling of the West (if you don't know anything, that's OK). Skim the chapters, looking at pictures, captions, and maps. In the "What I *Want* to Know" column, write three questions you have about the West. After you read the chapters, fill out the "What I *Learned*" column.

WORD BANK   capital   depression   range   longhorns   savages

Complete the sentences below with words from the word bank. One word is not used.

1. Another word for money is ___Capital___.
2. ___Longhorns___ were a type of cattle that were raised in the West.
3. The ___range___ is another name for the plains where ranches were located.
4. A ___depression___ occurs when large numbers of people lose their money or jobs.

CRITICAL THINKING   FACT OR OPINION

A fact is a statement that can be proven. An opinion judges things or people, but cannot be proved or disproved. Put F or O in front of the sentences from the chapter below from the chapter.

___O___ 1. Buffalo are dumb, but even if they'd been smart they didn't have a chance.

___F___ 2. The settlers had been fighting wars with the Indians since the Pequot War, back in Massachusetts in 1631.

___F___ 3. Plains farmers needed to be able to stand up to extremes of heat and cold, and to violent storms.

___F___ 4. Chicago was the nation's busiest port.

___F___ 5. The Texas longhorns were descended from cattle brought to America by Columbus and the Spaniards who followed him.

___O___ 6. And they were like knights: they rode with amazing skill, handled danger with bravado, and had their own code of honor.

___F___ 7. Cowboys were usually up before dawn and often hard at work into the night.

___O___ 8. Hickock was a sharp dresser.

MAP

Study the map from page 55. Complete the statements below.

1. Longhorns were driven ___North___ from ___Texas___ to ___Kansas___.

_____ (a) west, Kansas, Colorado _____ (b) north, Texas, Kansas _____ (c) east, Wyoming, Texas

2. The ___Goodnight-Loving___ Trail followed the ___Pecos___ River ___North___ to Cheyenne.

_____ (a) Goodnight-Loving, Pecos, north _____ (b) Chisholm, Red, east _____ (c) Western, Cimarron, north

3. Railroad lines ran ___Northeast___ from ___Dodge___ City through ___Kansas___ City.

_____ (a) south, Kansas, Dodge _____ (b) northeast, Dodge, Kansas _____ (c) west, Dodge, Kansas

4. The ___Union Pacific___ railroad ran ___North___ of the ___Santa Fe___ railroad.

_____ (a) Santa Fe, north, Union Pacific _____ (b) Union Pacific, north, Santa Fe _____ (c) Union Pacific, south, Santa Fe

RAILS ACROSS THE COUNTRY

SUMMARY *On May 10, 1869, the Central Pacific and Union Pacific lines met, adding new meaning to the name United States.*

ACCESS

This chapter describes the challenge of building a railroad across the United States. Copy the main idea map from page 8 into your history journal. In the large circle, write *Continental Railroad*. As you read, write facts about the challenges faced, the workers, the Indians, and the railroad tycoons in the smaller circles.

WORD BANK   visionaries   subsidy   meridian   contempt

Complete the sentences below with words from the word bank. One word is not used.

1. _Visionaries_____ are people who can imagine actual events in the future that many people doubt will actually happen.

2. A ___meridian_____ is a line of longitude found on a map.

3. A government ___subsidy_____ helped the railroad owners obtain land.

WITH A PARENT OR PARTNER

With a parent or partner, compare the map on page 62 with the map on page 55. Write the answers in your history journal. Where would Omaha be located on page 55? Where would Kansas be located on page 62? Where would the New Mexico territory be located on page 62? Where would the Missouri River be located on page 55?

CRITICAL THINKING   DRAWING CONCLUSIONS

Each of the sentences in *italics* below is taken from the chapter. Put a check mark in front of all of the conclusions that can be drawn from reading the lines.

1. *The country learned of the importance of railroads during that [Civil] war, when armies were moved by train.*

____✓ (a) Armies had not moved by train before the Civil War.

____✓ (b) Moving armies by train allows them to travel long distances faster than on foot.

_____ (c) The Confederates did not have railway lines.

2. *The Chinese worked incredibly hard, for long hours, and, mostly, were treated with contempt.*

____✓ (a) Chinese workers were critical to building the railroad across the U.S.

____✓ (b) White Americans were prejudiced against people from China.

____✓ (c) Building a railroad was difficult, exhausting work.

3. *When the transcontinental railroad was finished, Stanford, Durant, and the other railroad tycoons were national heroes.*

____✓ (a) Americans admired successful business leaders.

____✓ (b) Most Americans did not know how the tycoons treated their workers.

_____ (c) The tycoons were heroes to Native Americans.

WRITING

In your history journal, draw a scene from the descriptions of the West you have read about in chapters 11, 12, or 13.

TAKING THE TRAIN

SUMMARY *For passengers, traveling on the transcontinental railroad was one of the great experiences of the late 1800s. But for Plains Indians, the "iron horses" spelled disaster.*

ACCESS

This chapter describes a railroad trip across the United States in the 1870s. To help understand travel during this period, make a K-W-L graphic organizer in your history journal like the one on page 9. In the "What I *Know*" column write what you know about the first railroads across the U.S. (If you don't know anything, that's OK). Skim the chapter. In the "What I *Want* to Know" column, write three questions that come to mind about traveling by train in the 1870s. After you read the chapter, fill out the "What I *Learned*" column with answers to your questions and other information.

WORD BANK   transcontinental   emigrant cars   Pullman cars   iron horse   reservation

Complete the sentences below with words from the word bank. One word is not used.

1. Wealthy people who afford to pay for extra comfort traveled in _Pullman cars_.
2. _Iron horse_ was the name given by Native Americans to railroad trains.
3. People who rode in _emigrant cars_ sat on hard wooden benches.
4. A _transcontinental_ trip was one that went from one coast to the other.

CRITICAL THINKING MAKING INFERENCES

Put P in front of the words describe traveling in Pullman cars. Put E in front of the words that describe traveling in emigrant cars. Put B in front of the sentences that describe traveling in both the Pullman cars and the emigrant cars.

_P_ 1. The journey from Omaha to Sacramento will cost $40.

_B_ 2. The train will take you from the Eastern to the Western sea, and do it in only eight or ten days.

_E_ 3. There you'll sit—night and day—on hard wooden seats (without any padding at all).

_P_ 4. There you'll find fancy seats that convert into beds.

_B_ 5. Of course you will have to change trains in Chicago and again in Omaha and yet again in Ogden or Promontory, but that is all part of the adventure.

_P_ 6. . . . beautiful wood paneling, mirrors, reading lamps, carpeting and attendants to fuss over you.

_E_ 7. Don't worry, there is a stove to warm the car and an enclosed toilet and sink.

_B_ 8. . . . that makes the total cost of the trip $100, which is more than the average American workingman earns in a month.

WRITING

Study the drawings of train travel on pages 65 and 66. Imagine that you are either in an emigrant car or a Pullman car. In your history journal, write a postcard home to your best friend, telling in three or four sentences about the trip. Illustrate your postcard with details from the period.

FENCING THE HOMESTEAD

SUMMARY *Once settlers moved into the "Great American Desert," they used technology—windmills, barbed wire, and iron plows—to transform the environment into an agricultural region.*

ACCESS

This chapter describes life on the Great Plains as it was settled by immigrants. To organize your notes, make an outline like the one on page 8. For the title, write *Great American Desert*. For main ideas, write *Settlers, Farming, Climate,* and *Environment*. Write at least two details under each main idea.

WORD BANK   Great American Desert   Grange   barbed wire   sowing

Complete the sentences below with words from the word bank. One word is not used.

1. Another name for the prairie in the 1800s was the <u>Great American Desert</u>.

2. Farmers were able to keep cattle from trampling their crops after <u>barbed wire</u> was invented.

3. The <u>Grange</u> was an organization of farmers who worked to protect their interests.

CRITICAL THINKING MAIN IDEA AND SUPPORTING DETAILS

Each sentences in *italics* below states a main idea from the chapter. Put a check mark in the blanks in front of the ONE sentence that DOES NOT support or tell more about the main idea.

1. *Many homesteaders were immigrants—right off the boat.*

_____ (a) Some western settlements became all German, or all Danish, or all Swedish, or all Norwegian.

__✓__ (b) It wasn't an easy place to be a farmer.

_____ (c) Many immigrants tried to hang on to their original culture.

2. *In 1862 (which was during the Civil War), Congress passed a bill called the Homestead Act.*

__✓__ (a) Land in the East was spoken for.

_____ (b) It said that for $10 any citizen, or anyone who had filed papers to become a citizen, could have 160 acres of public land.

_____ (c) As soon as the Civil War was over, a lot people headed west to get land and become farmers.

3. *Self-sufficient farming wasn't suited to the Plains area or the times.*

_____ (a) In the 19th century, agriculture became a big business.

__✓__ (b) Now the cowboys had a problem.

_____ (c) Many farmers became specialists who grew only one or two crops.

WRITING

Think back to the chapters you have read so far. If you had lived in the 1870s, would you have preferred be a farmer or a cowboy (women were cowboys too)? Explain your choice in your history journal.

CHAPTER 16

REAPING A HARVEST

SUMMARY *The McCormick reaper did for farming what Eli Whitney's cotton gin did for cotton growing. It made big farms practical and profitable.*

ACCESS

This chapter explains how the invention of the McCormick Reaper brought enormous changes in farming. Review chapters 11 and 15 and make a K-W-L graphic organizer in your history journal like the one on page 9. In the "What I *Know*" column, write what you know about farming on the Great Plains after the Civil War. Skim the chapter. In the "What I *Want* to Know" column, write five questions you have about farming after the Civil War. After you read the chapter, fill out the "What I *Learned*" column with answers to your questions and other information.

WORD BANK   sod   reaper   scythe   installment buying   phenomenon

Complete the sentences below with words from the word bank. One word is not used.

1. Before the middle of the 1800s, a farmer harvested grain by hand with a ___scythe___.

2. Without trees to use for timber, settlers on the plains had to build their houses from ___sod___.

3. A mechanical ___reaper___ cost more than most farmers could afford at one time, so they purchased the equipment by ___installment buying___, paying a little each month.

CRITICAL THINKING FACT OR OPINION

A fact is a statement that can be proven. An opinion judges things or people, but cannot be proved or disproved. Put F or O in front of the sentences below from the chapter.

___F___ 1. John Deere designed a steel plow.

___O___ 2. But that was nothing compared to what Cyrus McCormick's reaper did.

___O___ 3. He rarely wasted time or played games.

___O___ 4. He was a business and marketing genius, too.

___F___ 5. In 1879 the McCormick factory produced 18,760 reapers; two years later it made nearly 49,000 machines.

___F___ 6. Because the country seemed so large, American farmers had always farmed wastefully.

___F___ 7. The Hatch Act established agricultural experiment stations in each state.

WORKING WITH PRIMARY SOURCES

Read the words of William Inge from Chapter 15, page 69. In your history journal, answer the questions that follow.

> The Plains States are the heart of our nation, and that heart beats slow and sure. . . . Nowhere can we find a closer correlation of landscape and character than in the Plains States. The people are . . . as plain and level . . . as the scenery.

1. Why does Inge call the Plains States the "heart of our nation"?

2. How did McCormick's reaper help make the Plains States the "heart" of the nation?

3. What does phrase "correlation of landscape and character" mean?

4. What do the words "plain and level" mean in describing people?

THE TRAIL ENDS ON A RESERVATION

SUMMARY *Native Americans found themselves pushed onto unwanted lands called reservations where they were expected to change into farmers or live on government handouts. The 1890 massacre at Wounded Knee marked the end of Native American hopes for autonomy.*

ACCESS

Make a cause and effect chart in your history journal like the one on page 9. For the first cause, write *Soldiers move west after Civil War.* For the first effect, write *Hostility between new westerners and Native Americans grows.* Follow up with at least four links in a cause-and-effect chain. Make sure to mention railroads, farmers, and cattle ranchers.

WORD BANK   ceded   extinction   abundance   compatible   maniacs

Complete the sentences below with words from the word bank. One word is not used.

1. An ___abundance___ is much more than enough.

2. The Indians ___ceded___, or gave up, their land during the 1800s as settlers moved to the plains.

3. Buffalo were hunted almost to ___extinction___; there were fewer than 100 left by the end of the 1800s.

4. Whites and Indians did live in ___compatible___ ways.

MAP

Compare the map of Indian lands on page 83 with the map of the Transcontinental Railroad on Page 62. Answer the following questions in your history journal. Then compare it with the map of the Great Cattle Trails on page 55.

1. Where did the railroad cross Indian land?

2. Where did cattle cross Indian land?

3. What states from the earlier maps were created out of land taken from the Indians?

Discuss and make some notes in your history journal.

CRITICAL THINKING SEQUENCE OF EVENTS

Study the timeline "From Jamestown to Wounded Knee" on page 88. Put 1, 2, 3, and so on in front of the sentences to describe what happened to Native Americans in chronological order.

___7___ At least 150 men, women, and children are massacred at the last battle between whites and Indians in North America.

___3___ The Bureau of Indian Affairs is formed.

___5___ Sitting Bull is victorious at the Battle of Little Bighorn

___8___ Southeastern tribes are relocated in the Indian Removal Act.

___1___ About 100 million Native Americans live in North America.

___6___ The Dawes Act prohibits tribes from owning land.

___2___ The Northwest Ordinance recognizes Native American right to land.

___4___ Congress reverses the Northwest Ordinance.

WORKING WITH PRIMARY SOURCES

Read the words of Chief Kicking Bird below. In your history journal, answer the questions that follow.

> The buffalo is our money. . . . Just as it makes a white man's heart feel to have his money carried away, so it makes us feel to see others killing and stealing our buffaloes, which are . . . given to us by the Great Father.

1. How would buffalo be like "money" to Native Americans in the 1800s?

2. Why would a white man's "money" have no value to a Native American?

3. Who are the "others" that Kicking Bird is referring to?

4. Who is the "Great Father" that Kicking Bird mentions?

THE PEOPLE OF THE PIERCED NOSES

SUMMARY *In one last bid for freedom, Chief Joseph led the Nez Perce on a desperate flight toward Canada. His eloquent appeal for justice on behalf of the Nez Perce confined to reservation has become a rallying cry for people of all races and backgrounds.*

ACCESS

Make a timeline graphic organizer in your history journal like the one on page 9. Begin in the year 1805 (what happened then?) and jump forward to four months in 1877, the end in 1904. Write down facts that you learn from the chapter and from page 93. Can you use information in the chapter to determine when Chief Joseph was born?

WORD BANK   rendezvous   bonanza   reservation   homesteaders

Complete the sentences below with words from the word bank. One word is not used.

1. A ___rendezvous___ is meeting between groups of people.
2. The ___reservation___, or land set aside, for Native Americans was usually barren and worthless.
3. The discovery of gold was a ___bonanza___ for white miners, and a disaster for the Nez Perce.

MAP

Study the map from page 93. In your history journal, answer the questions that follow.

1. About how many miles did the Nez Perce travel from June 12 (1 on the timeline) to July 11 (5)?
2. How many miles did the Nez Perce travel from July 11 to August 9 (8)?
3. What direction did the Nez Perce travel from August 9 to August 20?
4. How many miles did the Nez Perce travel from September 13 to September 30?

CRITICAL THINKING   DRAWING CONCLUSIONS

The words below in *italics* are words of Chief Joseph taken from the chapter. Put a check mark in front of all of the conclusions that can be drawn from reading the lines.

1. I claim a right to live on my land, and accord you the privilege to live on yours.

___✓ (a) The Nez Perce did not want to share their land with whites.

_____ (b) The Nez Perce did not want white to leave the land they had settled.

_____ (c) The Nez Perce were a warlike people.

2. You might as well expect the rivers to run backward as that any man who was born a free man should be contented when penned up.

___✓ (a) The Nez Perce did not want to be confined to a reservation.

_____ (b) The Nez Perce did not consider liberty a right for all people.

___✓ (c) The Nez Perce believed they had a right to freedom.

3. Whenever the white man treats the Indian as they treat each other, then we will have no more wars.

___✓ (a) The Indians wanted the same rights as the settlers.

_____ (b) Chief Joseph believed there would be no more wars.

___✓ (c) Chief Joseph believed that equal treatment would bring peace.

WRITING

What does the word *freedom* mean to you? What does the word *liberty* mean to you? In what ways are the words alike? In what ways are they different? If our county was founded the right of "life, liberty, and the pursuit of happiness," why did some settlers feel "free" to take the land of Native Americans? Write down your thoughts in your history journal.

A VILLAIN, A DREAMER, A CARTOONIST

SUMMARY *Bosses such as William Marcy Tweed built political machines that lay outside the system of checks and balances set up by the Constitution. Nonetheless, they found themselves checked by another nongovernmental power—the scathing pen of political cartoonist Thomas Nast.*

ACCESS

Make a K-W-L graphic organizer in your history journal like the one on page 9. In the "What I *Know*" column write what you know about city living today. (If you don't know anything, that's OK.) Skim the chapter. In the "What I *Want* to Know" column, write five questions you have about city living in the 1800s. After you read the chapter, fill out the "What I *Learned*" column.

WORD BANK   Tammany Hall   scoundrel   subway   political machine   graft   constituent   pedestrians

Complete the sentences below with words from the word bank. One word is not used.

1. Boss Tweed was a dishonest ___scoundrel___ who controlled an unofficial government known as a ___political Machine___ that was based in a club called ___Tammany Hall___.
2. A ___subway___ is a transportation line that runs underneath city streets.
3. A ___constituent___ is a person that a politician represents.
4. ___Graft___ occurs when politicians take advantage of their positions to make money.

CRITICAL THINKING MAIN IDEA AND SUPPORTING DETAILS

Each sentences in *italics* below states a main idea from the chapter. Put a check mark in the blank in front of the ONE sentence that DOES NOT support or tell more about the main idea.

1. *New York was home to more than 100,000 horses.*
_____ (a) Imagine all that manure spread around by wheels and feet.
_____ (b) When the manure dries it turns into powder that blows in your face and goes up your nostrils.
__✓__ (c) There were so many people that sometimes it took an hour just to move.

2. *Fresh air was the last thing Boss Tweed cared about.*
_____ (a) He was a scoundrel—a real bad guy who controlled most of the city's jobs and services.
__✓__ (b) Horses, people, buses, and carriages are pushing and shoving on Broadway.
_____ (c) He used his power to get money for himself.

3. *He decided to build a subway and not tell Tweed.*
_____ (a) He built it right under Broadway, and no knew he was doing it.
_____ (b) He invented a hydraulic tunneling machine and pneumatic subway.
__✓__ (c) He was called "Boss" Tweed and he ran New York City.

4. *Finally, the newspapers began writing editorials telling the truth about Boss Tweed.*
_____ (a) A cartoonist—named Thomas Nast—drew funny cartoons that showed Tweed as the wicked man he was.
__✓__ (b) It is about Ely Beach's fight with Boss Tweed.
_____ (c) When threats didn't work, Boss Tweed offered Thomas Nast half a million dollars to stop drawing his cartoons.

WRITING

Make a poster advertising Ely Beach's demonstration of the subway. Be sure to illustrate how Beach's subway works.

PHINEAS TAYLOR BARNUM

SUMMARY *"There's a sucker born every minute," is a saying people attribute to P.T. Barnum. Americans so enjoyed Barnum's form of hucksterism that he turned his Barnum and Bailey Circus into "The Greatest Show on Earth."*

ACCESS

To organize your notes about P.T. Barnum, make an outline like the one on page 8. For the title, write *P.T Barnum*. For main ideas put *Museum*, *Circus*, and *Popularity*. Put at least two details under each main idea.

WORD BANK   humbug   huckster   prohibition   bizarre

Complete the sentences below with words from the word bank. One word is not used.

1. A __Huckster__ is another name for a showman.
2. __Humbug__ is a hoax or a fake.
3. The law banning alcohol was called __prohibition__.

CRITICAL THINKING FACT OR OPINION

A fact is a statement that can be proved. An opinion judges things or people, but cannot be proved or disproved. Put F or O in front of the primary source sentences taken from the chapter.

__F__ 1. P.T Barnum admitted that he became famous fooling people.

__O__ 2. No one seemed to mind.

__O__ 3. But most people in America—after the Civil War—needed to laugh.

__F__ 4. He built a circus—the Barnum and Bailey circus.

__O__ 5. He called it "The Greatest Show on Earth," and, no doubt about it, it was.

__F__ 6. The star of Barnum's circus was an elephant whose name was Mumbo Jumbo—but everyone just called him Jumbo.

__F__ 7. P.T. Barnum got rich and built himself a fantastic home with pagoda-like wings and Gothic turrets.

__O__ 8. It was as bizarre as you would expect his house to be.

WORKING WITH PRIMARY SOURCES

Read the words of Hamlin Garland below. In your history journal, answer the questions that follow.

> [The circus] came from the east . . .filling our minds with the color of romance. It brought to our ears the latest . . . popular songs. It furnished us with jokes. It relieved our dullness. It gave us something to talk about

1. What do you think Garland meant in the phrase "color of romance"?
2. Who would "furnish" the "jokes" in the circus?
3. What do the words "relieved our dullness" mean in the phrase above?

WRITING

In your history journal, make an advertisement for one of P.T. Barnum's attractions.

CHAPTER 21

HUCK, TOM, AND FRIENDS

SUMMARY *In vivid prose, Mark Twain captured the dreams, schemes, and hopes of a people as he described everyday life in the closing years of the 19th century.*

ACCESS

To help organize the information in this chapter, make a main idea map in your history journal like the one on page 8. Put *Mark Twain* in the large center circle. As you learn facts about Twain write them in smaller circles.

WORD BANK   Gilded Age   sumptuous   exigencies   apprentice   segregation

Complete the sentences below with words from the word bank. One word is not used.

1. ___Exigencies___ are demands that require action
2. During the ___Gilded Age___ people were overly concerned with making money.
3. In summers, Twain ate large, ___sumptuous___ meals at his uncle's farm.
4. As a young ___apprentice___ Sam Clemens learned the printing business.

CRITICAL THINKING SEQUENCE OF EVENTS

The sentences from the chapter below are taken from Twain's life. Put 1, 2, 3, and so on in front of the sentences to put them in chronological order.

___3___ Or maybe it was because he ran away from the army during the Civil War and didn't want to get caught.

___5___ He called the book *A Connecticut Yankee in King Arthur's Court.*

___2___ In Hannibal, young Sam Clemens was apprenticed to a printer.

___6___ Mark Twain and his writer friend Charles Dudley Warner named the years after the Civil War the "Gilded Age."

___4___ The he drifted around the country, taking printing jobs in St. Louis, New York, Philadelphia, and Iowa.

___1___ I was born on the 30th of November, 1835, in the almost invisible town of Florida, Monroe County, Missouri.

___7___ Even when he was an old man—and looked like a polar bear—he could still think like a child, which isn't a bad thing.

WORKING WITH PRIMARY SOURCES

Read the description of a church by Twain below. In your history journal, answer the questions that follow.

> There was a log church, with a puncheon floor . . . made of logs whose… surfaces have been chipped flat with an adze. . . .In winter there was always a refreshing breeze through the floor; in summer, there fleas enough for all."

1. From the description of the floor's construction, what do you think an "adze" was?
2. What does Twain really mean when he says there was a "refreshing" breeze through the floor in the winter?
3. How do you know he is being humorous when he says there were "fleas enough for all"?

WRITING

Read about the meal that Twain describes on page 110. In your history journal, describe the biggest and best meal you have ever had. Write at least four sentences.

IMMIGRANTS SPEAK

SUMMARY *Although the Germans and the Irish made up the largest groups of 19th-century immigrants, the late 1800s saw a flood of newcomers from eastern and southern Europe. Their arrival fueled the growth of cities and industry, propelling the nation into the modern era.*

ACCESS

To organize the information in the chapter, make two cause-and-effect charts in your history journal like the one on page 9. For the first cause put "Revolution in Germany." What was the effect. For another cause, put "Famine in Ireland." What was the effect? Make three more links in a cause-and-effect chain.

WORD BANK   immigrate   emigrate   tenements   steerage   abysmal   famine

Complete the sentences below with words from the word bank. One word is not used.

1. _Tenements_____ were crowded dwellings in cities where immigrants lived.
2. People who chose to leave or _emigrate_____ from their homeland often had to travel in the hold section, or _steerage_____ of an ocean liner.
3. People who wanted to enter or _immigrate_____ into the United States often had to live for days below decks in awful or _abysmal_____ conditions.

WITH A PARENT OR PARTNER

Review the map and chart "Immigration 1860-1900" on page 114. With a parent or partner, discuss the following questions. Write your answers in your history journal.

1. In which decade did the most immigrants arrive in the United States?
2. From which part of the world did they come?
3. When did your family come to the United States?
4. From where?

CRITICAL THINKING MAKING INFERENCES

Put a check in front of the word or words that has about the same meaning as the underlined words in the immigrants' writing

1. One of our neighboring families was moving far away across *a great water . . .*
   _____ (a) the Mississippi River __✓__ (b) the Atlantic Ocean _____ (c) the Great Lakes
2. Does not American suggest a hot climate? These thoughts *consoled* me when I parted with my sheepskin coat
   _____ (a) disturbed _____ (b) angered __✓__ (c) comforted
3. [T]his is true Americanism, and to his I *pay the tribute of my devotion.*
   _____ (a) offer all of my money __✓__ (b) pledge allegiance _____ (c) pay ransom
4. We poor immigrants were *treated shabbily.*
   _____ (a) dressed in rags _____ (b) well cared-for __✓__ (c) neglected
5. Everyone on board was *jubilant.*
   __✓__ (a) delighted _____ (b) disappointed _____ (c) Jewish
6. Equality . . . is the great *moral element* of true democracy.
   _____ (a) missing piece _____ (b) illusion __✓__ (c) foundation

MAP AND CHART

Study the map and chart above. In your history journal, answer the questions that follow.

1. How did immigration change between 1875 when the first federal immigration restriction was passed and 1880?
2. From which part of Europe did most immigrants come between 1860 and 1900?
3. Which American country sent the most immigrants to the United States?
4. About how much did immigration rise between 1880 and 1882?

MORE ABOUT IMMIGRANTS

SUMMARY *Although most immigrants cherished American ideals, not all Americans welcomed them. The backlash against immigrants took the form of ugly ethnic, racial, and religious prejudice.*

ACCESS

This chapter discusses the arrival of immigrants in second half of the 19th century and the prejudice the many immigrant groups faced. To organize your notes as you read, make an outline like the one on page 8. Title it *Late 19th Century Immigration*. For main ideas, wrtie *Immigrant Needs, Prejudice Against Immigrants,* and *Chinese Immigrants.* Write at least two details under each main idea.

WORD BANK   prejudice   Know-Nothings   racism   anti-Semitic   exploiting

Complete the sentences below with words from the word bank. One word is not used.

1. People who "pre-judge" a group of people are displaying ___prejudice___

2. ___racism___ is a belief that people of a different race are inferior.

3. People who are ___anti-Semitic___ are prejudiced against people who are Jewish.

4. The ___Know-Nothings___ were a political party that was anti-Catholic and anti-immigrant.

CRITICAL THINKING   DRAWING CONCLUSIONS

Each of the sentences in *italics* below is taken from the chapter. Put a check mark in front of all of the conclusions that can be drawn from reading the lines.

1. *Usually the immigrants were poor, and willing to work hard and for less money than those who had arrived earlier.*

_____ (a) Immigrants didn't care about money.

___✓___ (b) Immigrants were willing take any jobs.

_____ (c) American workers feared losing their jobs to immigrants.

2. *The Workingmen's Party demanded a law to end Chinese immigration.*

_____ (a) Workingmen's Party members were not prejudiced against other groups.

_____ (b) Workingmen's Party members were white.

___✓___ (c) Workingmen's Party members felt that Chinese were taking their jobs.

3. *In 1882, American racists got a Chinese Exclusion Act passed.*

___✓___ (a) Senators and representatives voted for the racist act.

_____ (b) American racists were white.

_____ (c) The Exclusion Act kept out all immigrant groups.

WORKING WITH PRIMARY SOURCES

Read the words of the traveler Xu below. Answer the questions that follow.

> Talk about going to the land of the flowery flag made my face fill with happiness . . .
> Words of farewell were said to the parents, and my throat choked up.
> Parting from the wife, many tears flowed face to face.

1. What is "the land of the flowery flag"?

2. What do you think Xu did when he felt his "face fill with happiness"?

3. What do the words "my throat choked up" mean?

4. Why did tears flow "face to face" when Xu parted from his wife?

THE STRANGE CASE OF THE CHINESE LAUNDRY

SUMMARY *The Chinese in San Francisco felt the lash of prejudice when white law officials shut down their laundries. The fact that white-owned laundries remained open added extra sting to the injustice.*

GOING TO COURT

SUMMARY *The case of Yick Wo v. Hopkins revealed the power of the 14th Amendment. In a landmark decision, the Supreme Court used the equal protection clause to overturn the decision to shut down Chinese laundries.*

ACCESS

These chapters discusses an important case in which the U.S. court system protected a Chinese immigrant. To organize the information in the chapter, make a main idea map like the one on page 8. In the center, put *Lee Yick*. In the smaller, connected circles, put *Laws, Courts, People*, and any other important ideas that tell more about the case of Lee Yick.

WORD BANK

ordinance   naturalized citizen   nativism   Chinese Exclusion Act   appeal   criminal law   civil law   aliens   defendant   prosecutors   jurisdiction

Complete the sentences below with words from the word bank. One word is not used.

1. When Congress passed the ___Chinese Exclusion Act___ in 1882, it demonstrated ___nativism___ a belief that the United States was for whites only.

2. A ___naturalized citizen___ is a person born in another country who comes to the United States and files citizenship papers.

3. ___Civil law___ is law that deals with business or money matters as opposed to ___criminal law___ which usually focuses of crimes.

4. ___prosecutors___ are lawyers who prosecute people who they believe have broken an ___ordinance___, or law.

5. A ___defendant___, the person charged with a crime, can ___appeal___ a jury's decision and ask another court to hear the case.

6. Many Americans were prejudiced against ___aliens___, people who immigrated to the United States from other countries.

CRITICAL THINKING SEQUENCE OF EVENTS

The sentences below describe the events in the case of *Yick Wo v. Hopkins*. Put 1, 2, 3, and so on in front of the sentences to describe what happened in chronological order.

___3___ Chinese laundry owners went on trial, were convicted and fined in San Francisco court.

___5___ Lee Yick's appeal case was heard by the California Supreme Court

___4___ Lee Yick convinced other laundry owners to hire a lawyer to appeal the first court decision.

___8___ After the California Supreme Court agreed with the San Francisco Court, Lee Yick appealed to the U.S. Supreme Court.

___1___ Lee Yick immigrated to San Francisco and opened a laundry.

___7___ The sheriff and the states lost their case in the Supreme Court.

___2___ Yick Wo and other Chinese laundry owners are arrested by Sheriff Hopkins for violating an ordinance.

___6___ Briefs from other states supporting Sheriff Hopkins are presented to the Supreme Court.

WORKING WITH PRIMARY SOURCES

Read the words from the Supreme Court decision.

> For no legitimate reason this body by its action has declared that it is lawful for 80-odd persons who are not subjects of China to wash clothes for hire in [wood] frame buildings, but unlawful for all subjects of China to do the same thing.

In your history journal, rewrite the court decision above in your own words.

TEA IN WYOMING

SUMMARY *Wyoming led the way in granting the vote to women. When the United States threatened to deny the territory statehood unless it abandoned women's suffrage, a representative declared: "We may stay out of the Union a hundred years, but we will come in with our women."*

ARE YOU A CITIZEN IF YOU CAN'T VOTE?

SUMMARY *In the struggle for women's suffrage, leaders such as Susan B. Anthony risked arrest and trial for casting trial ballots. Others, such as Belva Lockwood, pushed themselves into law practice so they could defend women's rights more forcefully.*

ACCESS

To organize your notes from these two chapters, make an outline like the one on page 8. Title it *Women's Suffrage*. The three main ideas are *Suffrage in Wyoming*, *Susan B. Anthony*, and *The 15th Amendment*. Write at least two details under each main idea.

WORD BANK   suffrage   ~~veto~~   justice of the peace   ~~temperance~~   benign   impartial

Complete the sentences below with words from the word bank. One word is not used.

1. A president has the power to _____veto_____ or reject a bill passed by Congress.
2. Women were denied _____suffrage_____, the right to vote until 1919.
3. Some women fought for _____temperance_____, which means banning alcohol, because they did not think drinking was _____benign_____, or harmless.
4. A _____impartial_____ is a local official who has the power to marry couples.

CRITICAL THINKING   DRAWING CONCLUSIONS

Put S in front of the sentences below if the person supports women's suffrage. Pat A if the person is against women's suffrage.

__S__ 1. "Political bondage equals slavery."

__S__ 2. "I do not believe the state of Georgia has sunk so low that her good men cannot legislate for women."

__A__ 3. "Woman can't engage in politics without losing her virtue."

__S__ 4. "We may stay out of the Union a hundred years, but we will come in with our women."

__A__ 5. "The best women I know do not want to vote."

__S__ 6. "It is the sacred duty of the women of this country to secure . . . their sacred right to the elective franchise."

__S__ 7. "Yes, sir. I had resolved for three years to vote."

__A__ 8. "We, the people does not mean we, the male citizens."

WRITING

Imagine that you are a reporter in the gallery of Susan Anthony's trial by Judge Ward Hunt. In your history journal, write a headline and brief paragraph describing what happened and the reaction of the crowd in the courtroom.

28 MARY IN THE PROMISED LAND

SUMMARY *In her autobiography, Mary Antin gave a voice to the hopes, hardships, and dreams of many immigrants. For Antin, the United States was indeed The Promised Land.*

ACCESS

This chapter describes the immigration of a Jewish family to the United States through the eyes of a young woman. To organize the information in this chapter, make a cause and effect chart in your history journal like the one on page 9. For the first cause, put *Jews forced to remain behind pale.* For effect put, *Jewish shtetls develop.* Try to make at least three more cause and effect links in the graphic organizer.

WORD BANK   beyond the pale   shtetl   rebbe   gentiles

Complete the sentences below with words from the word bank. One word is not used.

1. People who act out the acceptable limits of behavior are said to be ___gentiles___.

2. A ___rebbe___ was a teacher in the Jewish village, the ___shtetl___.

CRITICAL THINKING   SEQUENCE OF EVENTS

The sentences below are taken from *The Promised Land.* Put *B* if Mary Antrim is describing a time before she came to the United States. Put *A* if she is describing time after she came to the United States.

__A__ 1. My father produced several kinds of food, ready to eat, without cooking.

__B__ 2. The last night at Polotzk we slept at my uncle's house.

__B__ 3. The first time Vanka threw mud at me, I ran home and complained to my mother.

__A__ 4. The door stood open for every one of us.

__A__ 5. A little girl from across the alley came and offered to conduct us to school.

__B__ 6. Not all the Gentiles were like Vanka.

__A__ 7. Education was free.

__B__ 8. Luxuries, such as schooling, had to be cut off.

WORKING WITH PRIMARY SOURCES

Read the words of Mary Antin below. In your history journal, answer the questions that follow.

> The essence of American opportunity, the treasure that no thief could touch, not even misfortune or poverty . . . I was thrilled with what this . . .freedom of education meant.

1. What does the word "essence" mean in the excerpt above?

2. What is the "treasure" that Antin is writing about?

3. Why do you think Antin felt that education kept her safe from "misfortune or poverty"?

4. Why was Antin "thrilled" about the "freedom of education"?

WRITING

Imagine that you are a student in the class that Mary Antin enters on her first day of school. Write a diary entry in your history journal about the new immigrants who came to school that day and what your impression was? How did they dress? Did they speak English? Were you helpful to them or did you ignore them?

ONE HUNDRED CANDLES

SUMMARY *The Centennial Exposition in Philadelphia in 1876 celebrated American ingenuity and inventiveness. The marvels unveiled at the fair foreshadowed even greater achievements to come.*

HOW WERE THINGS IN 1876?

SUMMARY *The ideal of "equality for all" still lay beyond the reach of many Americans. But the fact that the Constitution had endured the test of civil war convinced most people that the United States would continue to change for the better.*

ACCESS

To organize the information in these chapters, make a main idea map in your history journal like the one on page 8. In the center of the organizer put *1876*. Make smaller circles on the left for Chapter 29. Make smaller circles on the right for chapter 30.

WORD BANK centennial exposition exports imports stagnating middle class mansion

Complete the sentences below with words from the word bank. One word is not used.

1. _Centennial_, like the word "century," comes from a Latin word meaning "one hundred."

2. _Exports_ are goods sent from the U.S. to other countries.

3. _Imports_ are goods brought into the U.S. from other countries.

4. An _Exposition_ resembles a giant fair combined with a circus.

5. A _Stagnating_ economy is a time when people's earnings do not increase and there is a great of opportunity.

6. The _middle class_ was not poor, but it was far from wealthy.

WORKING WITH PRIMARY SOURCES

Read the words of William Dean Howells below. Answer the questions that follow.

> The Corliss engine does not lend itself to description; its personal acquaintance must be sought . . . of this ineffably strong mechanism . . .where the engineer sits . . .and touches some irritated spot on the giant's body.

1. What is the meaning of the word "lend" in this passage?

2. What is the meaning of "ineffably" in this passage?

3. How does Howells use words to make the engine seem alive?

4. What conclusion can you draw from Howells's description about the impact the Corliss engine had at the Centennial?

WRITING

In your history journal, design an advertisement for the Centennial. Be sure to include at least one of the attractions in your ad.

CHAPTER 31

THE WIZARD OF ELECTRICITY

SUMMARY *The "invention factory" of Thomas Alva Edison set the pace of change as the nation entered its second century. Edison combined genius with hard work to give Americans phonographs, moving pictures, electricity, and more.*

ACCESS

Review all of the timelines that you have compiled so far in your history journal. Combine them all into facts from the years 1830 to 1900. Try to name at least one event in every decade, whether it involves inventions, immigration, Indians, or politics

WORD BANK   Morse code   filament   telegraph   dynamos   boiler

Complete the sentences below with words from the word bank. One word is not used.

1. A ___filament___ is material that glows but does not burn in an electric light bulb.
2. ___Dynamos___ are giant machines that make and store electricity.
3. ___Morse___ ___Code___ is the communication system used by the ___telegraph___ .

WITH A PARENT OR PARTNER

Study the timeline "Some American Inventions 1830 to 1910" on pages 156-157. With a parent or partner, discuss the following questions. Write your answers in your history journal.

1. Which of the inventions is most important to your daily life? Why?
2. Which inventions were most important for people who lived in farming areas?
3. Which were most important for people living in cities?
4. Which helped people in both farming and city regions?

CRITICAL THINKING   FACT OR OPINION

A fact is a statement that can be proven. An opinion judges things or people, but cannot be proved or disproved. Put F or O in front of the sentences below from the chapter.

___O___ 1. Sometimes disadvantages can be turned into advantages.
___F___ 2. Edison spent only a few months in school.
___O___ 3. Thomas Edison was a lonely boy.
___F___ 4. So he invented a writing telegraph—a machine that wrote words, not just dots and dashes.
___F___ 5 For the next five years, he patented a new invention almost every month.
___F___ 6. On October 21, 1879, Edison took some of that thread, put it in a glass bulb, pumped out the air, and turned on the current.
___O___ 7. Edison must have done a lot of perspiring.
___O___ 8. Edison was our most gifted and famous inventor.

WORKING WITH PRIMARY SOURCES

Read the two sayings of Thomas Edison below. In your history journal, answer the questions that follow.

> The individual who doesn't make up his mind to cultivate the habit of thinking misses the greatest pleasure in life.

> Genius is 99 percent perspiration and one percent inspiration.

1. What is the meaning of the word "cultivate" in the first passage?
2. What is the meaning of "habit" in the first passage?
3. What does Edison mean when he says genius is mainly "perspiration"?
4. Did Edison consider the "habit of thinking" to be "perspiration" or "inspiration"? Explain.

CHAPTER 32

JIM CROW—WHAT A FOOL!

SUMMARY *Hopes of equality from Reconstruction were dashed by the decision in Plessy v Ferguson. The only victor in the case was vaudeville-inspired fool named Jim Crow.*

ACCESS

This chapter discusses rise of Jim Crow segregation in the South and its effect on African Americans. In your history journal, make a cause and effect chart like the one on page 9. For the first cause, write *Congress sends troops South.* List the effect. Fill in at least four cause-and-effect relationships with information from the chapter

WORD BANK   segregation   franchise   poll tax   Jim Crow   white supremacy   lynching   caste

Complete the sentences below with words from the word bank. One word is not used.

1. *Segregation*_____, the separation of the races, was a policy favored by people who believed in
   *white supremacy*_____, that is, that whites were better than blacks.
2. Southerners took the ____*franchise*_____ or vote from African Americans by forcing them to pay a
   ____*poll tax*_____ to vote.
3. ____*Jim Crow*_____ laws, named after a stage character, resulted in the hanging, or ___*lynching*_____,
   of blacks by Southern whites.

CRITICAL THINKING SEQUENCE OF EVENTS

The sentences below describe the events in the South from 1865 to 1900. Put 1, 2, 3, and so on in front of the sentences to put them in chronological order.

___7___ *Plessy v. Ferguson* was one of the worst decisions the Supreme Court ever made.

___3___ At first the Southern states passed terrible black codes that practically made black people slaves again

___2___ In 1877, when the army troops left, congressional Reconstruction was finished.

___1___ Years of congressional Reconstruction followed: many blacks got a chance to go to school, to vote, and to hold public office.

___5___ Without the vote, blacks were powerless.

___4___ White Southerners turned to backward-looking leaders.

___6___ Then Congress sent army troops south.

WORKING WITH PRIMARY SOURCES

Read the words of Frederick Douglass below. Answer the questions that follow.

> The problem is whether American people have . . .honor enough, patriotism enough, to live up to their own Constitution . . .We only ask that we be treated as well as those who fought against it.

1. What is the "problem" that Douglass is referring to?
2. What do you think Douglass means by "honor"?
3. How do you think Americans would "live up" to the Constitution?
4. Who is Douglass referring to when he writes of "those who fought against it"?

WRITING

Imagine that you are a Supreme Court justice in 1896. In your history journal, write a few short sentences giving your opinion about the question of separate but equal. Begin like this: "In the matter of *Plessy v Ferguson*, I must disagree (or agree) with my fellow justices. I hold this position because . . ." (Complete with at least three sentences.)

IDA B. WELLS

SUMMARY *Ida B. Wells shouldered responsibility at an early age—not only for her family, but for the African-American struggle for equality. She risked her life by refusing to abandon the struggle for justice.*

LYNCHING MEANS KILLING BY A MOB

SUMMARY *After slavery, one of the darkest blots on our history was the era in which vigilante justice killed thousands of innocent people. To effect change, Wells spread the word about crimes against black people and championed anti-lynching laws.*

ACCESS

To help organize your notes about Ida B. Wells's fight against the lynching across the South, make an outline like the one on page 8. Title it *Ida B. Wells*. For the main ideas, write *Young Ida*, *Adult Ida*, and *Lynching*. Put at least three details under each main idea.

WORD BANK   vigilante justice   anarchy   boycott

Complete the sentences below with words from the word bank. One word is not used.

1. A society without laws or government will fall into ___anarchy___.

2. People who took the law into their own hands were following _Vigilante Justice_, which was never just.

CRITICAL THINKING   MAIN IDEA AND SUPPORTING DETAILS

Each sentences in *italics* below states a main idea from the chapter. Put a check mark in the blanks in front of the ONE sentence that DOES NOT support or tell more about the main idea.

1. *But Ida. B. Wells was a newspaperwoman and she had no intention of looking aside.*

___✓___ (a) Lords and ladies and some of Parliament's leaders met Ida B. Wells.

_____ (b) So she wrote about the murders—which were called "lynchings."

_____ (c) She moved, she bought a gun, and she kept writing.

2. *Wells hired a lawyer and sued the railroad.*

_____ (a) The judge said she was right and awarded her $500.

___✓___ (b) But writing did not pay enough to allow Wells to quit teaching.

_____ (c) But the Chesapeake and Ohio Railroad appealed the case to the Tennessee Supreme Court.

3. *Between 1882 and 1930, 4,761 people were lynched in the United States.*

_____ (a) It happened in the North and West as well as the South.

___✓___ (b) The 14th Amendment guarantees all Americans the due process of law.

_____ (c) But most lynchings were in the South, and most victims were black.

4. *When the city of Memphis refused to even try to find Tom Moss's murderer, she told her readers to leave Memphis.*

___✓___ (a) In the West it was called vigilante justice, but it was never just.

_____ (b) Within two months, 6,000 people had left Memphis.

_____ (c) Then she organized a boycott: she told her readers to stop riding the streetcars.

WRITING

In your history journal, write a letter to the editor of *Free Speech* expressing with support for or disagreement with the boycott of streetcars in Memphis.

A MAN AND HIS TIMES

SUMMARY *Booker T. Washington placed economic freedom ahead of other types of freedom. His judgment grew out of time in which he lived—a time in which many African Americans in the South barely scratched a living from the land.*

ACCESS

To organize the information in this chapter, make a main idea map in your history journal like the one on page 8. In the center of the organizer put *Booker T. Washington*. Fill in smaller circles with facts about Washington. Try to estimate a year when the facts occurred.

WORD BANK   vocational   soil-exhausting crops   synthetic

Complete the sentences below with words from the word bank. One word is not used.

1. <u>Soil-exhausting</u> such as tobacco and cotton, made farmland worthless because the soil lost its nutrients.
2. A <u>vocational</u> school trained young men and women in a trade or skill to make it easier to find a job.

CRITICAL THINKING MAKING INFERENCES

Put A in front of the sentences below if they describes a time in Washington's life after he was educated. Put B if the sentences describe a time before he was educated.

__B__ 1. I was born a slave on a plantation in Franklin County, Virginia.

__A__ 2. He spoke so well that he often left audiences cheering.

__A__ 3. Washington was expecting "a building and all the necessary apparatus for me to begin teaching."

__B__ 4. In this cabin I lived with my mother and a brother and sister till after the Civil War, when we were all declared free.

__B__ 5. I had a feeling that to get into a schoolhouse and study in this way would be about the same as getting into paradise.

__A__ 6. One of the older students would very kindly leave his lessons and hold an umbrella over me while I heard the recitations of others.

__B__ 7. Booker went to work in a salt furnace.

__A__ 8. One man began to criticize Booker T. Washington's style of leadership.

WORKING WITH PRIMARY SOURCES

Read the words of Booker T. Washington below. Answer the questions that follow.

> There should be no . . . stooping to satisfy unreasonable whims of Southern white men, but . . . keep in mind the 200 years' . . . prejudice . . .which the ex-slaveholders are called upon to conquer.

1. What is the meaning of the word "stooping" in this passage?
2. What do you "unreasonable whims" might be?
3. Why does Washington say that prejudice has lasted "200 years"?
4. Restate Washington's thoughts in your own words.

WRITING

In your history journal, write two opinions. One should agree with Washington's opinion. The other should disagree, and say that "ex-slaveholders" must get rid of their prejudice immediately. Write at least three sentences supporting each opinion.

A MAN AHEAD OF HIS TIMES

SUMMARY *W.E.B. DuBois rejected Booker T. Washington's approach to change. In words similar to the civil rights movement of the 1950s, DuBois demanded nothing less than full equality.*

ACCESS

To organize the information in this chapter, make a main idea map in your history journal like the one on page 8. In the center of the organizer put *W.E.B. DuBois.* Fill in smaller circles with facts about DuBois.

WORD BANK   color line   anti-Semitism   civil-rights movement   ideals

Complete the sentences below with words from the word bank. One word is not used.

1. For DuBois, the ____Color line____ was a separation between whites and blacks that had to be broken.

2. DuBois spoke out against ____anti-Semitism____, which was prejudice against Jews.

3. DuBois's writings about race helped begin the ____civil-rights movement____ that grew in the 1950s.

CRITICAL THINKING MAKING INFERENCES

Put W in front of the sentences below if they describe Booker T. Washington. Put D if the sentences describe W.E.B. DuBois.

_W_ 1. But he also told white audiences that if blacks could have jobs and economic opportunity they wouldn't demand social equality.

_W_ 2. He wanted full equality.

_D_ 3. Some people say he was the father of the civil-rights movement of the 1950s.

_W_ 4. President Theodore Roosevelt invited him to dinner.

_D_ 5. They knew that he had been fired from some jobs and that he had money problems.

_D_ 6. He worked to bring the vote to women, he spoke out against anti-Semitism.

_D_ 7. All the newspapers agreed with him; so did most college professors.

_W_ 8. He didn't know how to work well with others.

WORKING WITH PRIMARY SOURCES

Read the words of W.E.B DuBois below. In your history journal, answer the questions that follow.

> We are Americans, not only by birth and by citizenship, but by our political ideals . . .And the greatest of those ideals is that ALL MEN ARE CREATED EQUAL.

1. What does DuBois mean that blacks are Americans by "birth and by citizenship"?

2. How are "ideals" different from "ideas"?

3. Why do you think DuBois chose "all men are created equal" for the greatest ideal?

4. Why didn't DuBois write "all people are created equal"?

37 END WORDS

SUMMARY *Although America was far from perfect at the end of the 19th century, it was headed in the direction of freedom and equality for all its citizens.*

ACCESS

Make a timeline from 1776 to 1900 that combines all of the information on timelines you have created so far. Divide it into segments as follows: 1776-1860 and 1860-1900. Mark off ten-year periods. List important events that have been described in the book in each decade.

WORD BANK   city on a hill   class distinction   sweatshop

Complete the sentences below with words from the word bank. One word is not used.

1. For America's founders, the United States was like a ___city on a hill___ that drew the first immigrant to the country.
2. The American ideal of equality meant that there was no ___class distinction___ between rich and poor or noble and commoner.

CRITICAL THINKING   FACT OR OPINION

A fact is a statement that can be proven. An opinion judges things or people, but cannot be proved or disproved. Put F or O in front of the sentences below from the chapter.

___O___ 1. There had to be a reason for the colonies to break away from England.

___F___ 2. Andrew Jackson came along and said, "Let the people rule."

___O___ 3. So government has to have keen ears.

___F___ 4. Susan B. Anthony was willing to stand trial because she believed women should be able to vote.

___F___ 5. A little girl named Mary Antin was brought to America because it offered religious freedom.

___F___ 6. Jews like Irving Berlin, George Gershwin, Aaron Copland, and Leonard Bernstein would soon be composing music.

___O___ 7. America wasn't perfect, but it certainly was heading in the direction of freedom, equality, and happiness for all its citizens.

WORKING WITH PRIMARY SOURCES

Read the words of Thomas Jefferson below. In your history journal, answer the questions that follow.

> The mass of mankind has not been born with saddles on their back, nor a favored few booted and spurred to ride them.

1. To what does Jefferson compare the "mass of mankind"?
2. To what does he compare the "favored few"?
3. Why didn't Jefferson write "the mass of men and women"?
4. Restate Jefferson's thoughts words in your own words.

IN YOUR OWN WORDS

In your history journal, write a paragraph that explains when your family came to the United States and how they ended up in the place where you live.

NAME _____

DUE DATE _____

What I Need to **Find**

I need to use:

☐ primary
☐ secondary

sources.

Places I **Know** to Look

Brainstorm: Other Sources and Places to Look

WHAT I FOUND

Title/Author/Location (call # or URL)

How I Found it

Suggestion	Library Catalog	Browsing	Internet Search	Web link

Primary Source
Secondary Source

Book/Periodical
Website
Other

**Rate each source
from 1 (low) to 4 (high)
in the categories below**

helpful   relevant

NAME _____

LIBRARY/ MEDIA CENTER RESEARCH LOG

DUE DATE _____

What I Need to **Find**

I need to use:

☐ primary
☐ secondary

sources.

Places I **Know** to Look

Brainstorm: Other Sources and Places to Look

WHAT I FOUND

Title/Author/Location (call # or URL)

☐ Book/Periodical
☐ Website
☐ Other

☐☐☐☐☐☐
☐☐☐☐☐☐
☐☐☐☐☐☐

☐ Primary Source
☐ Secondary Source

☐☐☐☐☐☐
☐☐☐☐☐☐

How I Found it

☐ Suggestion
☐ Library Catalog
☐ Browsing
☐ Internet Search
☐ Web link

☐☐☐☐☐☐
☐☐☐☐☐☐
☐☐☐☐☐☐
☐☐☐☐☐☐
☐☐☐☐☐☐

Rate each source from 1 (low) to 4 (high) in the categories below

helpful   relevant

LIBRARY / MEDIA CENTER RESEARCH LOG

NAME _____

DUE DATE _____

What I Need to Find

I need to use:

☐ primary sources.
☐ secondary

Places I **Know** to Look

Brainstorm: Other Sources and Places to Look

WHAT I FOUND

Title/Author/Location (call # or URL)

	Book/Periodical	Website	Other	Primary Source	Secondary Source	Suggestion	Library Catalog	Browsing	Internet Search	Web link	helpful	relevant

Rate each source from 1 (low) to 4 (high) in the categories below

helpful   relevant

How I Found it

☐ Web link
☐ Internet Search
☐ Browsing
☐ Library Catalog
☐ Suggestion

☐ Secondary Source
☐ Primary Source

☐ Other
☐ Website
☐ Book/Periodical

Title

Legend

Scale
0   200 m
0   200 km

Scale
0   100 m
0   100 km

W   N
S   E

Scale
0   150   300 Miles
0   150   300 Kilometers

US Relief Map

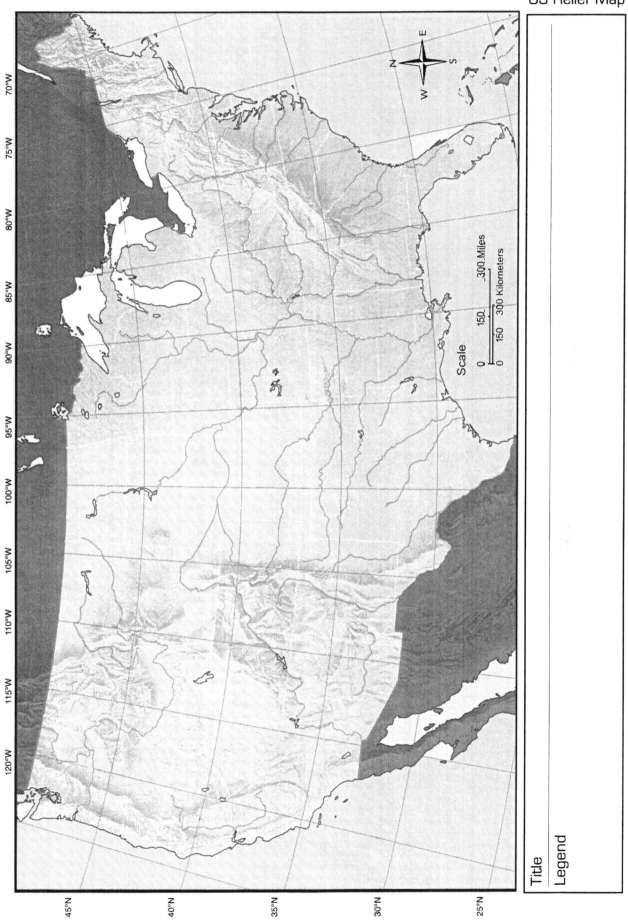

Title

Legend

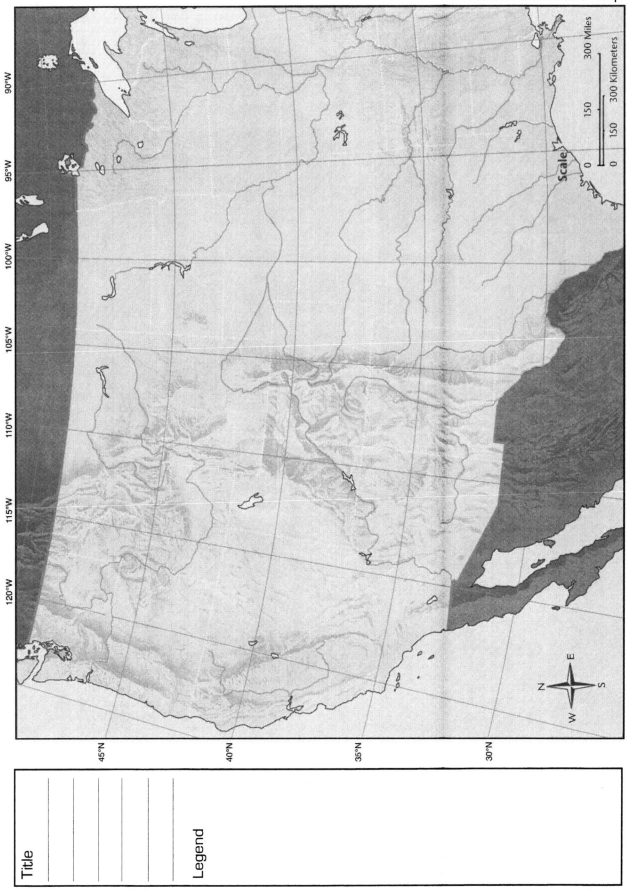

300 Miles

300 Kilometers

300

150

150

0

0

Scale

90°W

95°W

100°W

105°W

110°W

115°W

120°W

45°N

40°N

35°N

30°N

N
E
S
W

Title

Legend

Printed in the United States
R4555000001B/R45550PG135378LVX2B/1/P

Made in the USA
Lexington, KY
17 September 2010